PUSHING THROUGH

A.N. Bleakley

authorHOUSE®

AuthorHouse™
1663 Liberty Drive
Bloomington, IN 47403
www.authorhouse.com
Phone: 1 (800) 839-8640

Published by AuthorHouse 11/10/2017

ISBN: 978-1-5462-1591-2 (sc)
ISBN: 978-1-5462-1590-5 (e)

Library of Congress Control Number: 2017917005

Jeremiah 29:13 (NIV)

You will find me when you seek me with all of your heart.[1]

Contents

Foreword

In this moving narrative, my beloved and long-suffering wife reveals the impact on herself of the combined effects of my Asperger syndrome (probably inherited from my paternal grandfather, who was also socially inept and inconsiderate of my grandmother) and the demands of the Mormon Church in which I was raised.

Even as a child, I found that my behavior in social situations was often considered odd or unacceptable, and I tried to avoid social gatherings with unfamiliar people. The Mormon Church and the Civil Service both provided "safe" social scenarios, with clearly prescribed ways of doing things, speaking and acting. Just follow the formula and you couldn't go wrong! But put me in a nonchurch, nonwork gathering and I was totally at sea—and out of my depth too.

When I first met my wife, I found her refreshingly candid, intelligent, and honest, easy in conversation and sound in judgment. I proved to be a clumsy suitor, better able to communicate through letters than in person. I'm ever-grateful that, despite my inadequacies, she agreed to marry me and then to stick with me.

After a quarter of a century of married life I agreed to my wife's plea to attend a psychological assessment. Recounting some of my childhood gaffs assisted the assessor to confirm her diagnosis of high-functioning autism in the form of Asperger syndrome.

This was quite a revelation to my wife and helped her to understand some of the reasons for my odd behavior. Meeting other "Asperger wives" through the support group Cassandra confirmed this through shared experience. It is the spouse of the one with AS who is the sufferer, as this narrative explains.

Though the diagnosis gave an explanation, it did little to alter my behavior. My wife had come to the conclusion that Mormonism was far removed from the real Christianity she subsequently encountered. It took me another dozen or so years to wake up to the same conclusion. Leaving the Mormon Church after attending since early childhood, with fifty-five years on the books as a member, was life changing. My family and all my close friends were members. I was now adrift, without my familiar circle of friends or a rigid framework to follow. However, I now had permission to think for myself and to choose how to live, which was wonderfully freeing. My service in church is now something I choose to do.

I still fail to recognize social clues and tend to be somewhat obsessive, but I hope that I'm no longer so self-obsessed and can become more of a real partner to my dear wife as together we seek to follow the Lord.

Bob

There is about all complete conviction a kind of huge helplessness. A man is not convinced of a philosophic theory when he finds that something proves it. He is really only convinced when he finds that everything proves it. And the more converging reasons he finds pointing to this conviction, the more bewildered he is if asked suddenly to sum them up.[2]

—G.K. Chesterton

Prologue

An experience so significant and all-encompassing is hard to simplify but impossible to avoid. Well-worn clichés—the dawning realization, finding the missing piece, or the phrase "the empty cup now full"—come to life. Quite how it will be possible to describe the *everything else* C.S. Lewis referred to when he quipped "I believe in God as I believe in the sun, not because I see it rising but because by it, I see *everything else*"³ is bewildering.

Brad Kallenberg, in *Live to Tell: Evangelism for a Postmodern Age,* described the disjointed character of Augustine's memory of preconversion events. 'From a distance, his life looks like this: reads pagan literature [...]; idles away a year [...] studies rhetoric in Carthage; takes a mistress; fathers a child; teaches rhetoric; joins a cult; moves to Italy; studies philosophy; converts to Christianity.'⁴ Fads that characterized his early life were now seen as episodes in the single story of a life questing for God. He had discovered the gospel's power to knit together the disjointed phases of his life in such a way that he could perceive them as episodes in a story. He was graced with a new story that made sense of his past and, by joining its story line, invited him to shape his future. I share three of the last four features of Augustine's quest: after moving to Ireland, I joined a cult; studied philosophy, and converted to Christianity.

Getting the story right and learning to love the one true God is really about knowing freedom, ideologically speaking. I'll need help, so must trust the reader to be patient as I plunder the conceptual language of others. Kallenberg speaks of the acquisition of a new conceptual language. Of the acquisition of any language, he quotes George Lindbeck: "Just as one language may in the long term open up all the riches of human history and of a vastly promising though ominous future, the other, the better a child learns it, imprisons him more tightly in his little tribe or village."⁵

Chesterton's *it's only since I have known orthodoxy that I have known mental emancipation*[6] rings true for me too. What feels deliciously unique turns out to be no less deliciously universal—at least I'm assuming so for those aware they've been touched by the grace of God. It is the sense, to put it simply, that God can be a light in a dark place and that He really does have the whole world in His hands.

But first, as a trainee social worker, grappling with the idea of God, I joined the Mormon Church in 1977. It's probably truer to say that God was grappling with me. My slightly gray and unformed political views and the Church's practical Christianity seemed the perfect synthesis of religion and Marxist sociopolitical philosophies that were sociology's academic foundation. Stateside, it operated an impressive welfare program and provided members with optimum opportunities for service to the needy. It fostered an attitude of self-sufficiency and thrift and clear moral guidelines and looked very attractive—or "experientially relevant." In a society leaning toward religious disillusion and atheistic drift, it made belief in God respectable (or so I thought) and was the synthesis that I'd been, albeit unconsciously, looking for.

God *must* be the author of a faith that, counterculturally, showed all signs of dealing with issues of social need, yet not in a godless way, I reasoned. It was a "respectable" alternative to religion too heavenly to be of earthly use and of materialist social philosophy too earthly to be of real heavenly use. Despite its patriarchal structure, Mormonism had seemed democratic, ideologically utopian and organizationally sharp. Women enjoyed significant leadership roles within the organization while it reinforced the role of men within home and family life. It was hierarchical but in a curiously upside-down and classless sort of way. It also offered an alternative story.

But, in becoming a Mormon, as in Chesterton's delightful metaphor, I'd recognized the "treasures strewn from creation's shipwreck"—self-sacrifice, honorable service, ethical standards, and moral behavior—and had chased the treasures.[7] Carnell echoes this sentiment: "If a man deliberately followed this desire, pursuing their false objects until their falsity appeared and then resolutely abandoning them, he must come at last into the clear knowledge that the human soul is made to enjoy some object that is never fully given"—because God cannot give us peace and happiness apart from *himself*.[8]

Finally, the absence of peace and happiness that results from the pursuit of false objects is explained in the following excerpt: "a philosophical scheme that explains absolutely everything forces one to misconstrue even God as knuckling under to the system. Not only does an explanatory mode of philosophy wind up limiting God's freedom, and hence God's agency or 'personalness' but also, the success of any explanation of evil undermines the human need to repent; the more totalising the explanatory scheme, the less I am responsible for my actions."[9]

I was propelled by a longing for continuity, clarity, and healing and pursued them (and the collective unconscious) by returning in 1974 to my own—and Shaw's—now rather dreary "land of dreams." I'd been absent long enough to feel unhappily foreign, the result being a cautious, uneasy, and sometimes painful transition accomplished over a period of six years by a drip-feed strategy of progressively fewer absences and longer intervals. It was a surprise to Canadian friends who wondered why I was choosing to live with danger and the Irish political troubles. When my parents left Northern Ireland, it wasn't because they had anticipated the directional flow of Northern Irish politics or that Mum's mum would become the victim of a sectarian attack. She, along with seven other JPs, would have their homes bombed (all on the same day) by IRA incendiary devices when it was learned that they had signed summonses leading to the incarceration of nationalist suspects during internment.

Belfast, the city, was a new experience to me. It was never more than seventeen miles (or less than five) from where we had lived, but it had been far away from my childhood. Despite current political realities, my experience was that people cared for one another daily, confirmed in overheard snippets of conversation and by the variety of people who came to my grandmother's front door. There was in these people an underbelly of faith and delightfully little postmodern angst. They had views on the world, expectations of themselves and one another, a common cause, and a story. Neighbors regularly made use of Granny's telephone; policemen arrived with summonses to sign; there were visits from a cousin in Church ministry (a lay preacher), from his two impoverished spinster sisters, and from a minor political worthy or two. What need to explore the world when the world arrived as supplicant at your front door?

With the little influence in her small community, it was an ideal location for a political education and far more interesting and life affirming than life in the middle-class melting pot of North America. Mornings began with a rowdy dawn chorus: whistling milkmen and bottles clattering when set down by the doorstep, aromas of fresh bread from the local bakery followed by toast under the grill, tea brewing on the gas stove; the sound of Mackie's factory horn and hordes of men tromping purposefully to work. It strangely didn't matter if there was gunfire in the distance; Granny listened carefully, considering before making a dismissive gesture about the direction and distance *the rat-at*-at-tat was likely to be from her own front door. I'd returned to Ireland with a thoroughly postmodern mindset hungering to understand my own and my parents' personal histories. Since the war within me was arguably greater than the war without, I responded readily to the "treasures" of rootedness and continuity offered by life in Belfast, as well as Granny's magnificent storytelling that kick-started a genealogical odyssey that continues to this day. "What does my past reveal about who I am?"

If one could accept the touching testimony of the miraculous appearance of God to the humble farm boy Joseph Smith (and would *such* an organization, with *such* a historical pedigree promulgate *such* an extraordinary story if it were *not* true?), it would be less difficult to accept Mormonism's "fruits." Would thousands of sincere, self-funded young men forfeit two years of their lives to spread the good news if this was a fabrication? It would have to be a fabrication of extraordinary proportions. If membership statistics were any measure of their success, then the Mormon Church attracted a substantial and growing following—and could anyone argue with its evident good works? The core message was that we *do* what Jesus *did*: "These things ye have seen me do, do ye also."[10] If God desired that we love and serve one another, why wouldn't he direct an organization through a prophet through which we could become perfected in service? Wasn't the gospel story itself a *fantastic* one? If God could do what he did through Jesus Christ, couldn't he also do what Mormons claim he did through Joseph Smith? Appear? Direct an ordinary, imperfect man to set up an extraordinary church? If Joseph Smith's story was a fabrication, it was a fantastic fabrication that had produced a superior system for personal and social self-improvement and a politically conservative community of right-minded people.

Of course, God can do *whatever* He chooses to do through *whomever* He chooses in a way that is consistent with His will, but that, as it turns out, was precisely the point. "In the past, God spoke to our forefathers through the prophets [...] but in these last days He has spoken to us by his son."[11] God can break into our reality and intervene in our lives in mighty ways. The question was never "*can* God speak to us in these latter-days and if so, how?" It was and is "how does God continue to speak with us now as ever?" The possibility of God's miraculous interventions, coupled with the needs and longings of a human heart to know Him, lead the less discerning to the so-called certainties of counterfeit claims.

Whether deliberately or unwittingly, Mormons regularly fail to disclose Church teachings that are disturbing and that clearly place them outside the Christian tradition. Beneath the affable, families-are-forever image lies a disturbing pattern of cover-up, distortion, and misrepresentation. Joel Groat, of the Institute of Religious Research, states that "because most people with a Judeo-Christian background recognize the non-Christian nature of Mormon beliefs, there is immediate tension when these are introduced and at the same time that the claim to being a Christian church is affirmed."[12] He suggests that this tension is a catalyst for an increasingly dishonest portrayal of Mormon beliefs to the public in general and to potential converts in particular.

To minimize these, leaders omit disturbing teachings from official manuals, public discourses, missionary training, pageants, temple open houses, and official and unofficial websites. In addition to the aforesaid, a veneer of Christianity legitimized the claims for this less discerning convert—and the proof-texting of so-called latter-day scripture did the rest. This counterfeit "treasure" seemed a perfect story through which I could begin to shape my own. Like a story within a story, the universal and the particular, cosmic and personal, seemed at last to be coming together. As a religion it seemed, I suppose, sociologically respectable, and as I was evidently in want of a sociologically respectable miracle, I gave myself permission to believe.

For the time will come when men will not put up with sound doctrine. Instead, to suit their own desires, they will gather around them a great number of teachers to say what their itching ears want to hear. They will turn their ears away from the truth and will turn aside to myths.

—2 Timothy 4:3

Families Held Captive[13]

Arza Evans is a retired college professor from Utah who grew up thoroughly indoctrinated in Mormonism. He went on a full-time Church mission, served in several bishoprics, and worked in a Latter-Day Saints' temple. At about age forty, he began some serious research into early Mormon history that led to traumatic but liberating changes in his life.

The following comments from Arza Evans struck a deep chord with me:

> At first, the slogan "families can be together forever" may sound like a harmless, romantic notion; but in reality it is perhaps the most controlling and stifling doctrine taught by the Church of Jesus Christ of Latter-Day Saints. It creates fear of ostracism, closes minds, and regulates personal behaviour. Questions about this and other Church doctrine can cause serious family problems including divorce.
>
> A man or woman who comes to the conclusion that Mormonism is based upon deception and who then decides to leave the LDS Church must be willing to leave his or her family too. "It may turn out that the doubter is able to persuade some family members to change their minds about Mormonism but the odds are against this happening. The individual usually learns that family members have been so thoroughly indoctrinated that their highest loyalty is to the Church, not to a husband, wife, son, daughter or even to the truth; and a Church

member who associates or sympathises with an 'apostate' risks failing in his or her temple worthiness interview."[14]

This leads to a phenomenon known as "shadow Mormonism" wherein members secretly no longer believe but are "held hostage" due to family ties.

One shadow Mormon powerfully cried out on an ex-Mormon discussion board:

"To those of you on the outside reading this, please do not forget us. Please remember the hundreds of thousands of individuals currently serving life sentences in the prison of Mormonism. Please do not cease to pray to whatever god you serve for our deliverance. Some of us have no hope for redemption or liberation. For the greater good we sacrifice our souls upon the altar of conformity and orthodoxy. Our pain is real. Our sentence is absolute."[15]

Marriage

Bruce R. McConkie
Mormon General Authority

Being content to remain single in Mormonism was not an option. Marriage and family is central to Mormonism and has an extra meaning for Mormons. The church proclaims that the family is ordained of (commanded by) God and that marriage between a man and a woman is part of the plan of salvation and essential to His eternal plan.

Mormons see it as essential for salvation and believe that unmarried people cannot reach the highest level in the Celestial Kingdom after their death. They believe that the first marriage was performed by God and that the family unit will continue beyond the grave as a conscious, loving entity with the marriage partnership and parent-child relationships intact.

Mormons believe that God has ordered them to have children. This is so that spirits can spend a time of learning and testing on the earth in physical bodies. God's purpose for marriage is for a couple to have children and to teach them so that they are equipped to live the rest of their lives on the earth in physical bodies and then return to live with their Heavenly Father and Jesus Christ.

The most important single thing that any Latter-Day Saint ever does in this world is to marry the right person, in the right place, by the right authority. It is the gate to eternal peace and love here and eternal peace and love in the mansions on high.

A marriage can only last forever if it is performed in a Mormon Temple by a person with the priestly authority to do so. This ceremony is called "sealing" and takes about 20 minutes. After a husband and wife have been sealed in the temple, they must keep the covenants they have made and live the principles of love and obedience to achieve an eternal marriage. This means that they must love and be faithful to each other throughout their marriage and follow a course of Christian service throughout their lives. [16]

In addition, please note this comment from Prophet David O McKay regarding the necessity of bearing children: Any [...] desire on the part of a married couple to shirk the responsibility of parenthood reflects a condition of mind antagonistic to the best interests of the home, the state and the nation. No doubt there are some worldly people who honestly limit the number of children and the family to two or three because of insufficient means to clothe and educate a large family as the parents would desire to do but in nearly all such cases the two or three children are no better provided for than two or three times that number would be. Such parents may be sincere even if misguided; but in most cases, the desire not to have children has birth in vanity, passion and selfishness. Such feelings are the seeds sown in early married life that produce a harvest of discord, suspicion, estrangement and divorce. All such efforts too often tend to put the marriage relationship on a level with the panderer and the courtesan. They befoul the pure fountains of life with the slime of indulgence and sensuality. Such misguided couples are ever-seeking but never finding the reality for which their heart is yearning.

Quoted from 'Relief Society Magazine', Volume 3, No. 7, July 1916

Getting the Story Right

By now, I'd traversed the spectrum of psychological and social philosophy in an attempt to find that elusive "trail of meaning." Leading with its doctrinal claim to Christian origins, "experiential relevance" made Mormonism very attractive to me. It wasn't simply that people were generous and welcoming and cheerfully weary with well-doing, though that played a part; it was in their conviction that the Mormon Church's organization was itself divinely inspired. It was divinely designed to (ad)minister to the needs of its people. The distinction is subtle: to train them to do good works, using the most enlightened business practices of the latest Harvard Business School graduates in a *Seven Habits of Highly Effective People* way.

I had superficially prejudged the rightness of a doctrine, with its veneer of Christian orthodoxy, on the basis of its adherents' works. If I thought of doctrine at all, it was to conclude implicitly from what I'd witnessed the doctrine's coherence from its productive outworkings. Our wider views may indeed inform our smaller actions, yet the paradox is that our smaller actions do not necessarily reveal as much as we might think about our wider views. I hadn't seen that "if some small mistake were made in doctrine, huge blunders might be made in human happiness."[17]

Ravi Zacharias noted that for a doctrine to have validity, it must be ideologically coherent, empirically verifiable, and experientially relevant. In theorizing about the outworkings of Christian practice, interdependence and self-giving within a missional community were deemed fundamental to how we, as Christians, must be in community with one another.

Initially, faith in the system and Church hierarchy appeared to legitimize the godliness of my eternal partner, but increasingly I realized that it was my husband, a third-generation Mormon, and his family's philanthropic reputation that, in times of doctrinal dithering and doubt, legitimized the Church for me. The family's distinguished-service medals were never or rarely mentioned or used for social or political leverage, though some in the community may have balked at the weight this threw behind the cult of Mormonism and the establishment of a local branch of the Church.

My husband's family was kind, self-effacing, and rigorously ethical, as far as I could see (more "treasures" from that apocryphal shipwreck) and with such leverage in their kindness investments that their questionable affiliations were excused. Classless in social interaction, without sides, they inspired a remarkable degree of loyalty. So character became my signifier, and when life as a Mormon became difficult beyond description, I found it easier to blame my own inadequacies than to consider that my signifiers were deceived in their faith allegiance. Implicitly, the family's integrity, coupled with their longevity in the Church, legitimized the claims of the Mormon faith for me.

Mormon emphasis on family has a dark underbelly: if a person values family, that person will easily buy the spiritual blackmail that precious relationships will be lost for eternity unless he or she obeys Church rules. Mormons are taught to shelve doubts and to avoid feeding them with anti-Mormon literature. Indeed, current leaders have warned members that they should not study outside of the Church and should read only faith-promoting Church history. Most members refuse to look at problems for fear they would shake their testimonies of Mormon "truth." The fears that play a part in a Mormon's failure to resign membership include fear of damnation, loss of relationships, loss of business (in predominantly Mormon communities), loss of job (when employed by other Mormons), loss of reputation, and the fear that if Mormonism is not true, nothing else may be. It can feel psychologically, as well as spiritually, critical to shore up reasons to believe when, in times of doubt, there seems so much to lose.

> And it puzzles me to learn that though a man may be in doubt of what he knows
>
> Very quickly he will fight to prove that what he does not know is so.
>
> —Oscar Hammerstein, *The King and I*

My re-enlivened faith in God suffered as the Church insinuated its own agenda between me and any desire I might have had to deepen my knowledge of God or enter into a relationship with the Savior. Marrying and having children, or "eternal pregnancy," was a Mormon woman's preview of heaven. We perfected ourselves through obedience to Mormon principles: hard work prioritized on our behalf by the patriarchal priesthood order—what enlightened Christians might recognize as legalism with a difference. There was less and less time to question. "Trying is not sufficient. Nor is repentance complete when one merely tries to abandon sin. To try is weak," we were told. "To do the best one can is not strong. We must always try to do better than we can in every walk of life."[18] How often were we persuaded that the devil has work for idle hands? I believed I understood why pioneer wives might have accepted the idea of a polygamous "sister" to share the workload. There was little time for reflection, though reading the scriptures was a high priority on the list of evidences of faithfulness. In addition to preparing a weekly Church assignment were genealogy (redeeming the dead); writing a journal; planning and executing a regular family home evening; frugally baking, sewing, and knitting; attending to a vegetable plot and bottling, canning, or freezing its produce. Expectant mothers, weary with well-doing, discussed the value of cloth nappies over Pampers for a nest of children who were to be sung to, read to, taught the value of work, and organized in work projects to demonstrate to the modern world the benefits of an industrious pioneer heritage.

Church "callings" were offered as gifts or invitations from God through the inspiration of men to equip the humble for greater service. It was a humility measured by obedience to outer evidences of faith: regular attendance at meetings, tithing, temple worthiness, and general willingness to conform. Assigned speakers rode personal hobbyhorses, using supportive scriptures for effect. Members, constantly reminded of the rewards of faithfulness, strove to please the Lord by being obedient to men. The gospel turned out to be a business-style strategy for personal and social self-improvement with a veneer of Christian faith. There was little spiritual nourishment and lots of guilt.

I was thoroughly used up and should have asked, "Who am I really serving, and why?" much sooner. Mormonism had become the all-encompassing, total system that explained everything, and God had become the managerial systems man, whose revelation required organizational approval. He knuckled under. The effect was to distance God's authority and limit His freedom so that the language of Mormonism "imprisoned me tightly within my tribe and village."[19]

The few hymns that leaned toward grace and *God's* greatness focused my heart on Jesus, but we all missed the point of inviting Him to live there. We were too busy perfecting self to know Him or recognize that faith would be made perfect in weakness. Jesus was primarily the great exemplar, and we were to strive to do the things He did in obedience to His father. But we were to do the things He did *and* the things He was apparently telling us to do through His prophet.

At a crucial place, I arrived at a saving understanding of the significance of His sacrifice and my own sin. Righteousness was an imputed state. "God made Him who knew no sin to *be* sin for us that we might become the righteousness of God, in Christ."[20] When at last I asked Jesus into my life, I was enveloped by a peace that passed understanding and a love that enabled me to "see everything else"[21]: the Trinity, the cross, and the sufficiency of the Bible. God had been unwilling or unable to speak to me while I persisted in accepting an untrue picture of whom I worshipped. He *could* not give me peace and happiness apart from Himself.

I still had to untangle doctrinal heresies, but God's word sparkled, and I hungered for its nourishment and His continuing presence in my life. The universal and the particular had come together but that I had "sojourned long in Egypt" was never clearer. The realization came with a deep sense of loss "for the years the locust had eaten," and I felt acutely the consequences of having taught and raised five children—including two model missionaries—in the Mormon system. The sins of the parents: how to undo that?

Post-Mormon Feelings[22]

Arza Evans

The Keystone of Mormonism

When he finally became convinced that Joseph Smith was a clever con-man and that his Book of Mormon was not sacred ancient history but part of an ingenious mind game that he was playing with his gullible followers, this created some strong feelings in Arza Evans, many of which I share, and they are probably typical of other Post-Mormon truth seekers:

Fear

The first of my new feelings was fear. What will become of me? Will I lose my marriage and my family? And even if my wife stays with me, will she be angry and heartbroken? I was quite sure that my parents and my brothers and my sister would be either angry or heartbroken or both. Will I lose my job and have to move my family if I still have a family to move? Will they excommunicate me? (They did.) How many friends will I lose? Can I stand not being able to see my own children get married if they choose to get married in an LDS temple?

And what if I am wrong? Should I trust my own mind or just follow Church leaders? My parents and my brothers and my sister are intelligent people. Why don't they see the same deception that I see? Also, I am a fairly intelligent person. Why did it take me so many years to discover the truth? This is really scary. My eternal salvation may be at stake here! Should I bet everything I have on this or should I fold?

My fears were so strong that for a number of years I kept my true thoughts and feelings to myself. I became a "closet doubter." This was not good for my physical or mental health. But after all, how much should a person be willing to sacrifice on the altar of truth?

Fear is what keeps many people, even Church leaders, active in Mormonism. A woman friend of mine went to her stake president to get her temple recommend signed. He said, "Where is your husband?" She said, "He doesn't believe in the Church anymore." The stake president said, "Why not?" The woman said, "My husband started doing research into Church history and it made him see things in an entirely different way." The stake president said, "I know what you mean. I started to read *The Journal Of Discourses* and other Church history books. It nearly destroyed my testimony. I had to quit reading those things."

A good question for every LDS man and for every LDS woman to ask is, "What would I do differently in my life if I were not afraid?"

Sadness, Bereavement

Disillusionment with Mormonism has resulted in great sadness for me and for almost all of the other men and women I have talked with who have left the LDS Church. I think this bereavement has been even greater for me than the death of my parents. I don't know of one Post-Mormon person who started out to prove that Mormonism is not true or who has been gleeful with the results of their findings. The truth not only hurts, it is devastating! How can any active Church member really believe that one of their friends or relatives enjoys finding out that some of their most sacred and cherished beliefs are not true! And yet, there is no sympathy or condolence for the person suffering from this bereavement. Instead, Post-Mormons can usually expect anger and ostracism.

Confusion, An Upside-Down World

Moving away from Mormonism can turn a person's world upside down. At least that is how it has been for me. Things that used to bring me pride, now bring me shame and embarrassment. Instead of being proud that I sold my car and spent entire my life savings going on an LDS mission to the Chicago area (a very dangerous and tough mission), I deeply regret wasting two years of my life and all of my college money bearing my testimony about things that I now know are not true.

Also, I helped to break up a number of families when one person, usually the wife, became converted and then left her unbelieving husband. Naturally she wanted to find an LDS priesthood holder who would take her to a temple for an eternal marriage. I probably should have been horse-whipped by some of those angry husbands. I sincerely wish I could go back and change all of this, but I can't. All I can say is that I am very, very sorry.

I am no longer proud of being a faithful tithe payer. Almost all tithing goes for Church indoctrination programs, temple building, and missionary work. I no longer believe in these things. Very little tithing goes to help the poor.

I am not proud of being married in an LDS temple. I regret getting married in a place where Masonic rituals were presented as Christianity. I was told that learning these secret signs and passwords was necessary in order to pass by the angels and enter into God's clubhouse in the next world. Young family members, "unworthy" family members and "unworthy" friends were excluded from my wedding. An LDS temple marriage is not a celebration for the whole family. It is an occasion for ostracism of many family members. The Church is not family oriented but power oriented. It breaks up many families to enhance its power.

I am not proud of gaining my master's degree at Brigham Young University where the academic freedom of professors is very limited. LDS Faculty members need to pay tithing, have temple recommends, and carefully guard their comments in order to stay out of trouble. BYU is not widely respected in the academic world. I noticed a big difference when transferring to the University of Utah for further post-graduate studies.

My attitude toward my parents has also changed. Why were they so willing to indoctrinate me, a trusting little child, with Mormonism. Why didn't they ask a few open-minded questions and do some serious research? And why didn't they seem to have any questions about the temple rituals? In many ways my world has been turned upside down.

Anger, Betrayal, Entrapment

How is a person supposed to feel when she or he finally comes to believe that they and their entire family for generations have been duped by a very clever con-man? And what about all of those who have suffered and died on the plains and also those who have made great sacrifices in other ways for Joseph Smith's deceptions and myths? Are we to just look the other way and pretend that all of this pain and suffering never happened? This kind of spiritual deception is much worse than any stock fraud or pyramid scheme. It is passed on from generation to generation. The truth is that there never were any gold plates, Lamanites, Nephites, Jaredites, or Gadianton Robbers except in Smith's imagination. Once a person comes to realize this, he or she begins to feel like a gullible fool.

Powerful feelings of betrayal and entrapment emerge as a person begins to see the enormity of Joseph Smith's spiritual deception and the control of LDS entrapment. How can a person ever become free from this web of Mormon entanglement if a wife (or husband), parents, children, and grandchildren still belong to Joseph Smith and his Church?

The amazing thing to me is how much anger management and self control Post-Mormons seem to have. Perhaps this is because we have learned that prolonged anger can be self destructive and that forgiveness seems to be better for one's own physical and mental health.

It has always helped me with my anger management to realize that if there is an afterlife and a judgment day, then Joseph Smith, Brigham Young, and other false prophets and adulterers are now being severely punished by the Lord. But if there is no afterlife or judgment day, then these men have ceased to exist. They would have no way of taking any satisfaction in how wildly successful their deception has become.

It also helps me to realize that it took many years for me to finally see through the cunning dishonesty of early Church leaders. Then how can I expect better than this from others? Dreams die hard!

Happiness, Freedom, Exhilaration

After leaving Mormonism, many of us have felt a strong sense of freedom and happiness. A heavy burden has been lifted from our shoulders.

We can now read anything we want to read and do our own thinking. We no longer need to ask, "Does this information that I am reading go along with Mormonism? Is it faith promoting?" It doesn't matter any more. And, we can even choose our own underwear!

We are now free to respect the beliefs of other churches and religions and reject Joseph Smith's claim that the Lord told him that other churches were "all wrong" and that their ministers and pastors were "all corrupt." What deceptive nonsense this "revelation" was and is! How could I have believed this baloney for so many years? And post–Mormons no longer need to rationalize away or explain why over ninety percent of Joseph Smith's many prophesies never happened. The answer is obvious to an objective observer. Joseph Smith was a false prophet.

We no longer need to explain away or defend the immoral and illegal activities of Joseph Smith, Brigham Young and other Church leaders. These activities included money digging, an illegal bank, secret police (Danites) a private army (Zion's Camp), polygamy, and blood atonement. Involvement of Church leaders in the Mountain Meadows Massacre and other atrocities no longer reflect upon us Post-Mormons. We reject all of these things and the Church leaders involved.

We no longer need to explain away the many contradictions between Book of Mormon Mormonism and Nauvoo Mormonism. The overwhelming scientific evidence against the authenticity of the Book of Mormon including the Asian DNA of Native Americans is no longer our problem. But it is still a very big problem for LDS Church defenders.

We are also free from guilt for not attending endless meetings, and for not fasting, doing genealogy, temple work, home teaching, accepting all "callings," and confessing our personal lives to the bishop. We are free from the financial stress of paying tithing, and sending our children on missions. We are also free to spend more time with our families.

In the immortal words of Dr. Martin Luther King: "Free at last! Free at last! Free at last! Thank God Almighty, we are free at last!"

Note: There is no copyright on this paper (extract).

Autism Spectrum Disorder and Mormonism

For many years, I kept a poster published by the Samaritans. The advertisement showed a hand and face (mouth open) attempting to push through a clear plastic surface. It was an image evoking someone lost, trapped, and unheard. The caption read, "Is anyone listening?" For me the emphasis was on the word *anyone*. Anyone, anywhere.

Many years later, I saw that exact sentiment expressed in a chapter of the book by Karen Rodman *Is Anyone Listening?*[23] Rodman's compilation of essays and poems by the partners, parents, and family members of adults afflicted by Asperger syndrome (AS) suddenly gave voice to the feelings I'd had for many years. Had I been privy all those years ago to the particular difficulties I would encounter living with an AS adult, I doubt if I would have had the courage to continue. Only God can answer that question. However, in His faithfulness, God led me one careful step at a time into a deeper appreciation of my husband's genius, as well as giving me the grace to cope with some of the more exasperating character traits endemic to an adult with Asperger's.

We'd discussed children. Bob had grown up in a large, and from all reports, happy family and liked the idea of having six. I liked the *idea* too and felt sure that if we were to produce such a family we could do it together, successfully—with faith in God's help. I was confident that with this intelligent, godly man, we would put first things first and prioritize wisely. We would make time for each other, discuss difficulties, be united, and resolve conflict. We wouldn't knowingly misuse each other's time and would support one another's goals. Isn't that what marriage is all about? It seemed clear and safe to presuppose that having grown up in a large, happy family, the outworking of Bob's experience would be intuitive and that I could, in all probability, trust his judgment on most things. I was ready for children and felt confident that I had love enough for six. A broken family life had taught me the importance of consistency, clear messages, and keeping promises—also the importance of firm, clear boundaries, with occasional exceptions that wouldn't become the rule. To do this, we would be organized and work together.

I hadn't discerned that Bob's commitment to the rituals of church and tradition, skewed by the demands of Mormonism, would further skew his priorities and have an adverse impact on mine. I hadn't discerned that we were in fact, "divided by a common language." We used the same words, but they had different meanings. When I thought *God*, Bob thought *Church*, so to seek to know what God might want for each of us was translated by him as "what does the Church want me to do?" What I had inadequately understood as evidence of a transcendent relationship with a personal God turned out to be ritualistic obedience to outward forms that would tend to push us apart. Bob's commitment was to the more immediate and material demands of the Mormon program translated into meeting the exacting requirements of Mormon theology as mediated and designated by local Church leaders. We were continents colliding at the fault line, erupting at every attempt to draw close. The phrase "not singing from the same hymn sheet" comes to mind. Once he successfully added a wife to his program of activities, little changed. The busy life he'd known as a single man before marriage continued on much as before, though with the addition of a companion who was fitted in between meetings and projects. I'll admit to feeling very much like an add-on, another to-do (find and marry wife) on the list. But I believed that his affectionate assurances were evidence of sincere commitment to the relationship. Persuaded of this, I suggested activities we might do together. I knew Bob loved to sing, so I suggested we join a good local choir.

"No time."

Concert dates required rehearsal commitments, and it would be impossible to fit them in. I thought we'd both enjoy the local drama or operatic societies and have fun there too, but he said there would be too many performance rehearsals that would conflict with Church and other commitments.

"Cycling?"

He hated bicycles!

"Jogging?"

"Definitely not!"

"Couldn't you adjust your schedule?"

"Nothing I can change ... No, not really."

I was confused and hurt, as I'd been confident Bob had understood the "we" nature of marriage. He was a third-generation Mormon after all! Mormons "sold" the Church on the basis of what they presumed to know about marriage and families. Here was a caring and intelligent man who must surely understand that marriage was a together thing! It was irritating to find that if we did anything together, it would have to be Bob's things that we did—and when and where it suited him to do them. It seemed as though attendance at church meetings and socials would be, with few exceptions, the sum of all we would do. I felt cheated by what I considered at the time to be his selfishness and duped by what looked like self-interest posing as good works. I thought we'd agreed about doing things together and consulting one another about decisions. Had I misunderstood? Was "together" something a wife would facilitate by fitting in with her husband? His caring assurances drip-fed sufficient confidence in his good intent (if not his judgment) to persuade me that his priorities might, after all, be wiser than mine. Eventually I ceded to his judgment, as it was clear he'd been "called" to God's work. The leap to trust his judgment, too, appeared to be validated by the religious "call."

In the words of one expert, finding out your husband has Asperger syndrome is analogous to finding out your long-anticipated trip to Italy has been detoured to Holland. The idea is that Holland is simply a different kind of trip; if you spend the time despairing that it is not Italy, you will miss the joys of the windmills and tulips. The difference for the family of the undiagnosed adult with AS is to imagine that your trip to Italy is detoured to Holland, but everyone and everything there, including your relative with Asperger's, the tour guides, and the tour books, all insist that it *is* Italy. Your efforts to convince them that it is Holland are so confidently and authoritatively denied that you begin to doubt your own sanity. I couldn't know that he hadn't fully understood what "together" really meant, though I'd correctly sensed—as it turned out—he hadn't been knowingly dishonest.

The real agony of Asperger syndrome is suffered by the inner circle of family who bear the brunt of "emotional pain in this unrelenting abnormality."[24] Those afflicted by AS cannot relate to the pain brought upon their spouses, parents, children, or siblings. Often, the dissonance between how an AS-afflicted person interprets data and how their neurotypical [25] family members interpret the same data creates a disconnect that can be confusing and frustrating for everyone, especially in families where an AS-afflicted person has not been appropriately diagnosed. Rodman goes so far as to say that those "born with the affliction of Asperger syndrome survive at the emotional and psychological expense of others," although, "this is not done consciously on their part."[26] Those afflicted with AS often fail to comprehend what family members "are trying so desperately to convey." Their inability to respond emotionally to family members, especially a spouse, can be very frustrating for them. Rodman, in response to this frustration, asks a very pertinent question: "Where do we, the 'walking wounded,' go for help?"[27]

An Asperger's sufferer is almost certainly the wife of a charming, gifted, professional man. His "mild" eccentricities seem outwardly harmless. He can handle an astonishing amount of information (hard facts) accessed by his astonishing memory that absorbs the world through an astonishing eye for detail. He will confidently identify birds at distances I can just see or identify common as well as rare plants with their Latin names. He may write poetry, quote long passages from Shakespeare, recite an epic poem in its colloquial accent, sing, paint delicately in water colors, and become an expert very quickly in a subject it would take others years to learn. He may competently plumb his own bathroom or wire his house's electrical system or build a study or a cabin bed with such an eye for detail and finish that it leaves you to wonder. He might also design a clever, previously unheard of but useful gadget. The man's a treasure—give me six!

What isn't seen, except by someone in a close relationship with an Asperger man, is that the quantity of information and competencies that might make him a first-class employee or information resource exclude the possibility of a proper relationship. It's as if the spaces in the mind where relationship competencies should be are either filled with other information or are inadequately shaped to contain the necessary information. There is no room for social (or emotional) discernment, compassion, or empathy. In the absence of these vital human functions, emotional inaccessibility prevails, as well as an inability to anticipate or recognize that others have feelings. This lack of discernment, compassion, and empathy lead inevitably to the misinterpretation of intentions, lack of remorse, egocentricity, and rigidity. Whatever excludes reciprocity in a relationship clearly points to the inability to maintain one. It is a relationship disorder that makes life with an undiagnosed adult painful and frustrating. Distraught relatives are often blamed for the problems.

It might be thought that someone rigid, egocentric, and emotionally inaccessible, unable to empathize or recognize others' feelings, would be simply boorish—the ultimate chauvinist. Well, yes and no. No, because he is well-intentioned, charming, speaks quietly, and would rather leave a room than participate in contentious debate or engage in argument. He would be genuinely wounded at the suggestion that he had been hurtful, callous, or rude. Yes, because the effect of living with someone who knows everything, corrects everyone, and never makes a mistake feels a little like what it must have been to live on the receiving end of a certain patrician style of colonialism. He is a gentleman, but his (gracious) way is *the* way. There is only one way. His understanding is the correct and often only one, his decisions and motives wisest and best.

In relationships, people intuitively use relational antennae to understand how friends and loved ones feel and think about things—that's empathy. What is, I think, vital to the mental and emotional health of most of us, a healthy interest in and enjoyment of other people, appeared to be an unnecessary, if not expendable, element in Bob's. I write using the past tense because during this period of our lives, we had not yet discovered what AS entailed. Neither of us had any idea of how to surmount the gulf between my expectations and Bob's inability to perceive and interpret my hopes and assumptions. Perhaps more importantly, neither of us had yet experienced the spiritual regeneration that comes with accepting the Christian Godhead as one God in three persons: Father, Son, and Holy Spirit. The changes these two factors have introduced to our lives are greatly evident, but that story will develop with progress.

Bob lived for tasks; the farther away the tasks were from ordinary people, the better he could get on with them, undisturbed. This lack of emotional connection, combined with his general lack of curiosity or need for social engagement, created an aching sense in me that something in the relationship was not right.

In truth, nothing in Bob had changed or "died" at all, but a vital part of me *was* dying. The tasks Bob performed were for the benefit of others— indeed, everything he did was for the benefit of others, despite the fact that he was never truly *available*.

Production of children as a strand in the "fulfilment of tasks" worldview, devoid of intimacy or "soul," in time made our marriage disappointingly, alarmingly mechanical. Here, the Samaritan picture poster ad resonates most personally with my own state of mind. The unidentifiable person whose desperation, but not her face, is imprinted in the gray plastic is a frightening image: lost, trapped, unheard, and unrecognized. Is anyone listening? Anyone, anywhere? How very like the nightmares I had had as a child, both expressing an unnamed fear. I spiraled down and down, feeling myself fearfully driven toward a precipice where I would finally be reduced to a soulless cog in a very large Orwellian wheel.

For those wishing to find out more about the Families of Adults Afflicted with Asperger's Inc. (FAAAS) website, follow the endnotes link. [28]

Linguistic Gymnastics

Meetings were unavoidable. There were few evenings without meetings—work meetings, lectures to the Worker's Educational Association (WEA), Horticultural Society meetings, weekly church meetings, monthly church meetings, and home-visiting meetings. At work, while assisting with a legal case, Bob was called in for an extra evening, sometimes two, each week over a period of two years. His record-keeping was meticulous and helped the DOE's legal case. My appeal for relief from some of his many absences was considered "irrational." His extra activities took up next to no time at all! One evening for the WEA, one for the Horticultural Society, one for a monthly leadership meeting, one for home teaching, etcetera—as if one evening for each diminished the sense that he was doing too much. But Bob wasn't doing too much. Bob's schedule was perfectly manageable—for Bob. What I hadn't understood was that I hadn't spelled out the problem with the literalism his Asperger understanding required. Bob's schedule wasn't manageable to *me*. He wasn't doing too much; he was doing it in the "wrong" places—away from home.

What seemed like perversity and wordplay to manipulate circumstances and justify the priority of his own agenda was, unknown to me, an authentically arrived at conclusion based on how Bob heard and understood the world. If I said, "You are doing too much," I really meant "You are away from home too often and we're not coping well with your many absences." Bob heard, "You are doing too much" and replied, "No, I'm not." He was right that he wasn't doing too much. He could quantify what he was able to do perfectly well.

Adam Harbinson's book *Savage Shepherds* [29]details the excesses of the Shepherding movement once espoused by Deryk Prince, and others, though Deryk subsequently disassociated himself from the movement.

Whereas the Shepherding movement wasn't an actual cult, it displayed a few similar characteristics to the man-centered organizational structure of Mormonism:

> The busier we were kept, the less likely we would be to engage in any meaningful activities outside the orb of the fellowship. And so our lives became increasingly bound up in fellowship activities that separated us from the real world in which it was normal to ask questions. In such circumstances, you can lose touch with reality; the weird can become the norm.[30]

The confusion generated by the demands of living trustingly within an as-yet undiagnosed Asperger relationship was exacerbated by the demands of living obediently within this man-centered organizational structure. Within Mormonism, women are required to defer obediently to their priesthood-holder husbands, and I was sincerely trying to do both. At that point, I hadn't really come to grips with the fact that Mormonism's mind-control could qualify it as a cult, yet Harbinson's message resonated with an inner part of my being that recognized that the weird had become the norm in my spiritual life.

Prediagnosis, it was a game of cat and mouse. Bob never lost his temper but successfully "played" with mine. I found the linguistic gymnastics necessary to successfully communicate a clear message thoroughly exhausting. With a cryptic-crossword mentality, he answered straightforward questions in such convoluted ways that bridging the divide seemed, at times, entirely hopeless. He was a master at obfuscation and vague, noncommittal mutterings; I was usually trying to find a concrete plan to hold him to.

I once arrived home from a meeting to find that Bob had abandoned his children to fulfil an overdue church assignment, leaving the eldest, age ten, in charge. He arrived home looking very pleased that he'd managed to fit in yet *another* assignment so cleverly that he'd been barely missed! He'd been ticking his "good works" boxes doing something good for others! With a smile and self-satisfied flourish, he then handed me a bar of my favorite chocolate, leaving me speechless. Bob, however, was wounded that

I hadn't appreciated his good intent. It was beyond my comprehension. On the one hand he was an intelligent, caring man, but on the other he was irresponsible and childlike. If intelligent, I reasoned, he was dishonest and crafty—manipulative even, to slip out in my absence and then schmooze me with chocolate on his return. I couldn't trust him with responsibility because despite extracting assurances that there would be no "next time," there was *always* a next time. Bob would justify the fact that there really had been no next time due to there being few consistent variables linking one event to another.

He had an extraordinary ability to miss the unifying theme and to see the different variables in what were, to me, identical scenarios. It led me to think of him as deliberately perverse. I performed linguistic gymnastics in attempts to make the big picture yet more clear and to help him join the dots—but without success. Still, conversations would go off on irrelevant tangents as he locked on to a particular point and spun it as far away from relevance as it would go. I wanted to talk about reliability, or keeping his word, or not moving the goal posts, or knowing what to trust. He'd respond by telling an anecdote about an obscure incident so far removed from the context I'd be cross-eyed, scratching my head. Whether it was in the timely collection of our children from school or the promise not to disturb sleeping children with an electric DIY drill, in Bob's strange world of fulfilling his duty and being helpful, not only could he not respect boundaries or keep promises, but he was, in his own opinion and to my great frustration, never wrong.

The scenarios were reenacted like in the film *Groundhog Day*. The main character finds the events of each day repeating exactly as before. He has the same conversations with the same people at the same time and in the same place. He can anticipate what will happen and who will say what but can change nothing. He becomes agitated—desperate—and tries to find someone with whom he can share his point of reference. The needle is stuck on déjà vu.

Bob wasn't entirely unaffected by my descent into clinical depression, but he went on smiling at the world, doing jobs and being "helpful." When he appeared to have got something wrong, he could "try harder." But, as he was always well-intentioned, never planning to cause upset, he couldn't be wrong, and my unhappiness was, sadly, my own problem. Somewhere in this ideational mishmash, good intentions equaled righteousness—or "sinlessness." It resulted in his enviably self-assured and supremely confident take on life. Bob was always calm and reasonable, and I was reluctantly carried along by his self-confidence and his incredulity that I should think him cruel or unkind. He might be unreliable, irresponsible, or devious but he was always innocent because well-intentioned. It was a rather controlling game of mind-bending one-upmanship that I was entirely unable to get a handle on. In my mind, our relationship was not about winning or competing or relational one-upmanship; it was about working together for the good of all of us, whereas I felt exploited. In truth, I was also disorientated and confused by the guileless mixed messages, and so I hung on stubbornly to the few threads of reality left in my surreal universe. Counselors were not equipped to deal with the unique features of Asperger and neurotypical marriage partnerships at that time, so counseling did nothing for our relationship other than kick-start my personal psychotherapeutic odyssey.

I was on duty all the time, it seemed, for fear that Bob would drop the ball. I hated having to second-guess if he'd collected a child from school or Cub Scouts or an outing, as promised. I had to check up on him, which was entirely necessary. Had he forgotten? Frequently! Sometimes he hadn't been able to get to where he was meant to be on time because he'd had to finish some other more important task first. In discussions, he agreed that his child's well-being was more important than a piece of paperwork or a hastily arranged meeting, but there was little change in the outcome—although change is what I expected as a result of our postmortem resolutions. What a blessing mobile phones have been! Prior to this great tool providing us with immediate communication, there seemed little choice but to accept an excuse and trust that he really would follow through next time.

Was he really at home babysitting when he was supposed to be? Had he actually settled the little ones at a respectable hour? I was picking up the slack on jobs I'd delegated to Bob when picking up the slack in other areas of our life had been the reason to ask for his help in the first place. I didn't trust the excuses or feeling like a patsy to a confidence trickster; eventually it was impossible even to trust the good intentions. What could be relied on? Were lapses of memory due to the stress of demands on his time? Did skewed priorities reveal a weak sense of responsibility? The demands, or rituals, Bob seemed to think unavoidable were not helpful to our family. Though he asked to be reminded of family commitments, it confirmed that they were not his priority and that I had another dependent on whom it was necessary to check. *Our* time was effectively *his* time, and I had little choice in how it was used.

But Bob avoided difficult issues, as well as any suggestion he might have had anything other than good intentions. It somehow seemed more important to him that I understood he didn't mean to do whatever it was than it was for him to realize that his tendency to overwork and neglect his family caused upset and worry. "Not meaning to" was the answer to every problem, and with depressing regularity it continued to be the same answer to the same problems, over and over again. With astonishing and bizarre regularity, Bob would drop the ball: he would fail to collect the children; fail to deliver one or other to school on time; fail to warn any of us about expected lateness—or that he might not be home at all; fail to remember not to do noisy DIY at night; fail to pass on messages about births, deaths, or marriages; fail to remember not to correct me in public. But he successfully remembered quantities of obscure details that were not at all connected to the world I thought we lived in. He might be able to absorb the world through an astonishing eye for detail and handle an astounding amount of information in his extraordinary memory, but he was unable to collect or deliver his children to school on time.

The most difficult of the aberrations were the silences—those blank spaces in our conversations. What had happened to the long passages of poetry during courtship or discussions following visits to the theater? I could deal with the fact that there were fewer of those intimate moments now, but I struggled to accept that our conversations froze. In truth, there was an avoidance of exploratory or evaluative discussion on every subject, and though he had an astonishing memory for other things, he couldn't remember conversations or their tone. He was unable to discern the subtext in any social situation. Most communications were propositional—pronouncements and statements of observation—and related to the material, concrete world.

He observed and commented on the "needing to be done" factors in my day-to-day running of the household, which to me, implied dissatisfaction.

Attempts to preempt this by improving my home organization didn't work. He assured me that he intended no criticism, but there was *always* more to do that I'd missed, so he stayed up late to "help me" finish. As this was embarrassing, I worked harder and faster to get more done—laundry hung or put away, dishes properly stacked, etcetera—rather than have my husband stay up late, but I didn't have the stamina to do enough. There was always something undone that he found to do. On the rare occasion that I exceled and anticipated an evening at home with a hubby not busying himself with unfinished tasks, he went out because he had nothing to do!

There were always jobs to do, people to visit, tasks to perform, real or imagined obligations to others, and worthy reasons to justify it all. He could not simply *be*, or so it seemed, with me. Frenetic activity was directed to some other purpose, justified by yet another worthy cause. I felt lonely and overwhelmed, whether I kept trying or did nothing at all. I was also exhausted and fighting depression. Eventually, I stopped trying to beat the clock. If running the housework race gave Bob reason to be absent, my stopping running the housework race might give him a reason to stay home. I'd rather he was at home doing "unfinished jobs" than duty-bound to look for employment elsewhere. It didn't always work, especially if there was a meeting to attend, but it helped to ensure that he couldn't justify going out to help others quite so easily.

We'd had two children in nappies at one stage, followed by a few months respite before the next child arrived. Nappies were washed and hung. No wasting of electricity using the profligate clothes dryer! Everything was done the hard way, including avoiding prepackaged food. We grew our own fruit and vegetables and fixed and mended rather than replaced items. We felt very virtuous indeed. We worked at exemplifying a self-sufficient community in miniature, cooking and baking and sewing my heart out, with children helping—sort of. We had work time, playtime, clean-up time, and dinner time, followed by bath- and bedtime, after which I collapsed into a chair. Having resorted to stealth to keep Bob at home, we captured him for bed and story time, but small giggling children were often still awake in the wee hours. While Mum dozed downstairs in a chair, Dad had fallen asleep, midsentence, on the bed.

Our idea of being involved in social-circle engagements didn't gel either. When people came to visit who Bob didn't know well, he was likely to disappear into the garden. It was embarrassing and stressful not to be able to anticipate what he was going to do next or to know if I had his support in the hospitality department. I was usually already feeling that I simply wanted to go into a quiet room and read a book, but making an effort in social situations seemed rather fundamental. Unfortunately, I had to instruct Bob on what *not* to do to save my blushes before people arrived. It took so much energy that it became a disincentive to entertain at home; instead I chose to lunch with friends. That's about it. If and when Bob chose to remain in our company and not disappear into the garden, he wouldn't initiate conversations. He would find a way of entering in by pedantically correcting my use of English grammar or by nit-picking details in my conversation—any detail would do.

I found myself struggling to complete a sentence without interruption while he hovered at my side as I chatted to the women rather than engage members of his own sex in conversation. Knowing he was gearing up to find a detail to correct, I couldn't relax in conversation, anticipating interruptions. Showing how clever he was at my expense made me very cross, especially as I didn't feel I could defend my supposed grammatical sloppiness or lack of clarity without creating a competitive and graceless undercurrent. So I conceded—but seethed—and then spoke to him quietly after the incident, rather than embarrass him in public. I waited a very long time for the same courtesy to be reciprocated. Friends are much too important and necessary to risk a public scene that would send them running permanently. Sharing a sister-in law's facetious and even cynical sense of humor and similar experience was a form of salvation that made me braver and bolder. I felt able to share with select people the nature of Asperger's as it manifested in Bob. It made the few social events we enjoyed together considerably easier. Intelligent, discerning friends overlooked mannerisms and "absences," rescuing awkwardness with kindness and grace.

Bob (a.k.a. Mr. Spock) doesn't seek or understand the emotional, bonding function of communication. Bob's communication is practical and functional. Communication outside three-dimensional material reality doesn't make sense. Correction is therefore necessary. In reality, Bob is "helping"—to the point of distraction—and cannot seem to grasp that such "help" is far from welcome. He is, in fact, so competent at nearly everything in the three-dimensional world that it is impossible to argue that his input hasn't made things better. Having established his competence in many other areas, it is difficult for him to understand that he lacks innate competence in the more esoteric and intuitive fields. Having little or no insight into the social and emotional world, he imagines achieving competence is merely a case of trying harder—though what it is he is to try harder at is a bit of a mystery to him. It can be stifling and undermining to be supervised and quizzed or to feel like Eliza Doolittle[31] to his absent-minded Professor Higgins,[32] but he genuinely likes the comparison.

Bob still disappears without letting others know where he's going or how long he's likely to be. His mobile is likely to be switched off; he will arrive home late with an excuse about why he is late *this* time, resentful if his "legitimate" excuse isn't accepted. There will always be a reason, and the reason will have no connection to the previous reason. Hence his reasoning that each "lateness" is different from the last; the obdurate inability to recognize that "lateness" itself is a problem—his problem. If others depend upon my timekeeping, which might at times depend upon Bob's reliability, it can be a bit of a nightmare, frankly. I'd arrange a contingency plan to deflect the likelihood of being late in some future situation, but his irritation at not being trusted would lead him to prove me wrong by being on time! It was, confusingly, easier not to expect punctuality; Bob would be punctual only if I made it clear I didn't expect it. It was a tiring, perverse, and very silly game. Bob refused to recognize or admit that he played it.

He became angry and childishly stamped his foot if expected to change a routine, but there would be no response at all to a more critical breach of personal boundaries. He would use an electric drill for DIY in the evenings once the children were asleep or when I went to bed and then be annoyed when asked to stop—which he wouldn't. He would come to bed at four in the morning insisting he *had* been quiet so *couldn't* (!) have woken me. (In other words, I was suddenly awake at four in the morning for reasons other than that he had woken me.) Though I would ask that he use the spare room rather than risk waking me, that would then present him the challenge of proving he could come to bed in the wee hours without waking me up. Having woken me during one of these self-imposed challenges, he claimed it was the first time he'd failed all week (it was all about him, you see) or however many days he'd succeeded without actually waking me up. But he missed the fact that the request was not about proving to his own satisfaction how quiet he could be until the next time.

As Bob was usually home on a Saturday, I would try to fit one of my own church visiting callings into our frenetic schedule. I became anxious about leaving him in charge of the children after relatives who'd come to stay were alarmed to find my three-year-old jumping off the kitchen table while the others scaled the cupboards for biscuits as substitutes for breakfast. He was in the garden, oblivious to the possibility that intervention or supervision might be necessary. His logic was that he was there if *they* needed him.

There were very few friends I could confidently land four children on all at once, but occasionally Bob's mum would kindly sit with the children, as would Bob himself, if I had to attend a meeting. I wasn't confident that they would get to bed on time, but I urgently needed a break, and I reminded him of the routines, trusting and hoping the children wouldn't be in bed too much later than usual.

My anxieties about the children's safety left him unmoved as far as I could see. Once I accepted his reasons and acknowledged that I knew he didn't mean to cause distress or hurt, he would continue on where he had left off, as though his acknowledgement *alone* meant the problem was solved. I would (again) attempt to explain that the problem wasn't solved and we would soon be back where we'd started: another critical slip-up for yet another good reason and a promise to try harder next time.

Discussions took us around in circles, so examining the whys of Bob's frequent disappearances simply didn't work. He was usually well meaning and did not deliberately intend to give me reasons to be upset, but he left no room for discussion to defuse these issues; he couldn't understand that it wasn't his intentions that caused the problems. As far as he was concerned, if his intentions were faultless, there wasn't very much more he needed to do. I grabbed any available moment (with or without children present) to talk about something that couldn't wait, but often he wouldn't answer or would simply blank me out by continuing where he had left off. He went on reading the paper or listening to the radio or eating his meal, with a provocative lack of visible acknowledgement that I'd even spoken. Then he would go to a meeting or disappear to the garden while I was left feeling entirely powerless. *Is anyone listening? Anyone, anywhere …*

We always seemed to be at the same place as far as Bob's understanding of the children's or even his own boundaries was concerned. He couldn't impose boundaries on children or infer learning from one event to another because he didn't like the unpleasantness he seemed to think was associated with discipline. He would undo groundings or provide withheld pocket money. The children received pocket money when they shouldn't or were permitted to attend parties when the privilege had been withdrawn. He "forgot" boundaries we had previously agreed to, though these would be discussed in the same way over and over again, with little evidence of real understanding. It all contributed to my increasing sense of a loss of control. Our four small children could, as children do, opportunistically exploit the inconsistencies and differences between us.

As I already had to do most of the parenting, Bob's "well-meaning" sabotage of what had begun as consistent and predictable boundaries with our children caused me more than a little despair. Anxious conversations after each event on the effect of his "interventions" often ended with his comment that he understood *this* time and that he would try harder *next* time. What did he *mean,* try harder? Surely this was simply a case of do it or don't do it? Trying didn't come into it. It was beginning to sound like the same old song. It was inauthentic. It lacked meaning, conviction, and sincerity. Whether being consistently late, waking the family in the middle of the night, interrupting me midconversation, inappropriately and pedantically correcting my grammar in public, or sabotaging discipline and boundaries, "trying harder next time" sounded like the same old rhyme or formula that he used in a convenient and expedient way for evading consequences when he sensed himself in a tight spot.

On the face of it, Bob seemed to agree with the idea of boundaries. He'd get to bed on time or be polite in conversation, but in practice he simply didn't know what boundaries were, what they meant, or how to shape them. But the damage was done. The system broke down, and the children played on our inconsistencies. I pride myself on managing to keep consistent boundaries in the early days and in Bob's absence. However, the truly diabolical result of getting him to stay home more frequently and to be on board as a parent was creating an incomprehensible degree of disorder, unpredictability, and confusion that unraveled me. Suddenly, Bob's "help" added the equivalent of any toddler's good intentions to the mix. Though I'd seen it coming and had tried to stop it, life was spinning out of control, and I didn't know what to do. I was hanging on tightly to a quickly spinning roundabout, trying not to fly off into oblivion. I blamed myself for my failures.

It wasn't just that I needed an extra pair of hands—we had an *au pair* one summer and foreign students for two consecutive years providing help and companionship. There was simply no family life outside Mormon Church fellowship, just as there could be no *real* family life in it. There could *be* no real meeting of minds if there was avoidance of any opportunity to foster *this* meeting. The more I accommodated and submitted to the status quo at my own expense, the more avoidant[33] Bob became. Again I blamed the schedule, and I appealed to church leaders to release him from church obligations. However, the advice to make a date (an appointment!) with my husband each Friday night seemed bizarre, self-serving, and ignorant. I couldn't be sure who was colluding with whom or if anyone was any more in touch with the reality of the situation than I was myself, but as I was tired and scared and empty, perhaps it was me? I was unable to tell if it was the Mormon Church and its endless meetings and programs or if it was Bob and his insatiable busyness, using the Church programs to provide an outlet. But (in this instance) I suppressed the anger I felt when it was inferred by the Church's priesthood authorities that in my circumstances it was indelicate to complain. A line from Adam Harbinson's *Savage Shepherds* eloquently depicts my frustration at that time.

> [T]he single common factor was the effect of a hierarchy
> that created an elite group of people whose influence it
> was difficult to defy. [34]

According to the particular hierarchy to which I was in submission, I was, after all, very fortunate; I had, after all, many reasons to be grateful.

But another factor played a not-insignificant part in the relational unravelling. In Asperger relationships, the neurotypical partner's tendency to eradicate emotionality and take on Asperger's characteristics has been described as becoming *Aspergated*.

Failure to understand and validate legitimate emotional experiences or behaviors in one's significant "other" exacerbates negative emotional arousal in the invalidated individual. Potentially, this leaves each member of the relationship displaying some measure of dysregulated affect. [35]

Minimising the impact on a person who is in a relationship that is emotionally threatening perpetuates the problem when it should make us question. Under such conditions, it is far easier to believe survivors are "catastrophising" their perception of reality. These are the types of arguments perpetrators make to those they are abusing in order to hide and justify the abuse. It is an effective tool for silencing victims. [36]

—Lola Okolosie

Gaslighting

Oh God, make me like Spock. Purge me of emotion. Oh my soul, shut the "hell" up so that only my brain will speak and my heart will sleep a thousand years.[37]

Writing for the *Guardian*, Ariel Leve described the term *gaslighting* by comparing it with what she proposes is the American experience of making sense of the incoherent utterings of the current president. They must attempt to decipher what she believes that she, as a child, experienced frequently—that "nothing means anything and reality is cancelled."

Leaving aside the article's views on the current American presidency, the term *gaslighting* comes from the title of a Hitchcock film in which the heroine is manipulated into questioning and second-guessing her own reality. Facts and truth were discredited, and the question of how it was possible to know what to believe was thrust mercilessly into the foreground. When gaslighted by someone who is expected to embody both ethics and etiquette, the effect is certain disorder and confusion.

Describing a world in which there had been no emotional safety while being constantly told that she had a happy childhood and that she was ungrateful, what Leve had been exposed to, *as well as* her feelings about it, had had a verifiable origin. She had been on the receiving end of inappropriate behavior, but her reality was denied when she spoke the truth. What *was* she complaining about? What she had seen and experienced hadn't, apparently, happened. "She would say that I was making it up, that it was a lie. When I confronted her with facts, they were batted away. So it wasn't just that my reality was cancelled, but that my perception of reality was overwritten." [38]

The effect of gaslighting is to feel as though the ground is always shifting beneath you. There is no center of gravity. While being told up is down and black is white, the only way to make sense of it is to remain resolute. When someone is so certain about what they believe and they insist and keep trying to convince you, over a period of time it erodes your own perception. Having constantly to verify reality is, in itself, destabilizing.

I could say a hearty "Ditto!" regarding such childhood experiences with my own mother, but if there is any truth to the idea that human beings unconsciously replicate early experiences in later relationships, then "repetition compulsion" may have led me to my husband. It's unclear if the author of the above article views her experience of having been gaslighted by her mother as *intentional* on her mother's part. It may have been. But since her story means to describe how chaotic it felt to be on the receiving end, intent for this purpose is irrelevant. Barring intent, I suggest that the effect of being on the receiving end of gaslighting as described here is really not much different from the effect of being a neurotypical (NT) marriage partner in an Asperger (AS) relationship.

In *Solutions for Adults with Asperger Syndrome,* Juanita Lovett refers to Dr. Marcel Just's observations on cognitive brain imaging. His findings referred to the AS brain's "cabling' and underconnectivity." "The research finding of insufficient connectivity and poor integration between different brain areas suggests weak central coherence. The lack of connectivity and problems with integration would probably interfere with the AS brain coordinating and integrating the different kinds of information necessary to get the gist of a situation."[39]

This is key to understanding the map of Holland analogy, which I believe is worth repeating here: that finding out your husband has Asperger syndrome is analogous to finding out your long-anticipated trip to Italy has been detoured to Holland. The difference for the family of the undiagnosed adult with AS is to imagine that your trip to Italy is detoured to Holland, but everyone there, including your relative with Asperger's, the tour guides, and the tour books all insist that it *is* Italy. Your efforts to convince them that it is Holland are so confidently and authoritatively denied that you begin to doubt your own sanity. Holland is simply a different kind of trip, and if you spend the time despairing that it is not Italy, you will miss the joys of the windmills and tulips.

There's a familiarity and also, bizarrely, a sense of safety in relationships that *feel* in some way familiar (even in a form we do not understand and cannot quite see) that may nevertheless be quite unsafe. It was Bob's cryptic-crossword mentality, wherein straightforward questions were answered in convoluted ways, the obfuscation and vague, noncommittal mutterings within the hyperbusy day-to-day press of family life when a concrete plan was needed. It was an inability to grasp the unifying theme or to see different variables in what were identical scenarios. My own expectation of promised *leadership* (priesthood leadership) with clarity was set beside the lack of discernible boundaries and the gymnastic linguistic dance needed to successfully communicate a clear message. The game of cat and mouse was mentally exhausting. Karen Rodman titled her book *Is Anyone Listening?* and rightly asked "Where do we, the 'walking wounded,' go for help?"[40]

I agree with the writer's lament that one of the most insidious things about gaslighting is the denial of reality. Being denied what you have seen, being denied what you have experienced and know to be true, can make you feel crazy. Speaking once again about her mother, Levy said that it wasn't just the lack of boundaries or inappropriate behavior that did the real damage; it was denial that the incidents had ever occurred. The erasure was worse than the abuse. When there is someone you are afraid to lose, their insistence that *their* reality is *the* reality can often cause you to doubt what you know to be true. Second-guessing ourselves, we turn our attention to self as the person to blame.

A strategy that helped Leve survive was to become hypervigilant about clarity. Needing certainty in an uncertain world, there was simply no room for misunderstanding and no margin for error. People can give up their reality in favor of hanging on to a relationship rather than rupturing it. If you know something is true and you are told it's not true, holding on to your reality is essential. This, too, was, and is, vital to me.

Resonances

On the face of it, apart from other "Cassandra" wives of Asperger men, few people would not consider this the selfish tirade of a spoilt, ungrateful woman. The sufferer, they might think, is really *not* the wife but the Asperger man. He is, after all, a gifted, competent professional with a few endearing eccentricities, and—given the plusses of talent and good intentions—the man's a treasure. We really should have one each. But after all I've said thus far, you might be shocked to think I almost agree. If I can use the analogy that suggests the trip to Italy has been detoured to Holland, I've discovered that I'm happy to be in Holland once provided with a competent road map: a diagnosis. Negotiating Holland with a map of Italy had exasperating comedic moments, but it was never going to work. Like finding windmills and tulips where Rome was supposed to be and flat land on the site of Mars Hill, the delight is lost in disorientation, the inevitable mistrust of your own senses, and fear you're going mad. Unable to make sense of the map, you rage at the landscape.

Twenty-seven years on, with children grown and crises survived or averted, I'm like the Velveteen Rabbit—limp and shapeless, with my ears loved off. I will never be the same, but my heart's still beating, and I've been surprised at how quickly I've come to appreciate the windmills and tulips. I can separate my dear hubby from the syndrome. I understand what it might mean to have no "theory of mind" or "central cohesion." It is astonishingly liberating—if a study in confusion—but I love this sweetly kind man who is, apart from his demon (and the LDS Church) really very nice indeed.

Digging Out the Words

For what it may be worth, this has been my effort to make sense of two overriding and lived narratives in my life for twenty-seven years. The first is my marriage to an Asperger man, and the other is what that has meant (experientially) within a Mormon version of reality.

But I've arrived at the end of this narrative, grateful for my Asperger husband's encouragement to write. I was, in any case, bursting with a story that was desperate to emerge. I had (and *have*) no desire to wound or embarrass him. While he proofread and formatted much of what I've written, I've no sense or sign that any of it has caused him distress. While this suggests confirmation of much thus described, for *me*, his easy acceptance of its truth is confirmation that I am, in my *own* brokenness, loved.

"There is something about writing that can introduce us to ourselves and to the one in whose image we are made. Writing is helpful because the eye in the writer seeks the transcendent moments where the extraordinary is beheld in the ordinary glimpses of clarity within the junkyard—the beauty of God in a godless world.

For the past decade, doctors and psychologists have been taking notice of the health benefits of reflective writing. They note that wrestling with words to put your deepest thoughts into writing can lift your mind from depression, uncover wisdom within your experiences, provide insight, and foster self-awareness. Similarly, a recent news article discussed the benefits of confessional writing where one is freed to "explore the depths of the emotional junkyard." While writing is no doubt a helpful way to sift through the junkyard, its effectiveness is perhaps dependent upon learning from reflection, not merely reveling in the messes.

I have dared to utter the words at the center of my soul, and, in a sense, God has used my own pen to probe the wounds. In the intimate descriptions of life recorded in the Psalms, the writers of the Psalms express loneliness, joy, even frustration with God. "What gain is there in my destruction, in my going down into the pit? Will the dust praise you? Will it proclaim your faithfulness?" (Psalm 30:9.) Yet the psalmists walk away from their words with a clearer sense of reality; their words have been a source of encouragement to countless lives, uniting us to wisdom, to reality, and to the God enthroned on high.[41]

"In the C. S. Lewis novel, *Til We Have Faces*, the main character, Orual, has taken mental notes throughout her life, carefully building what she refers to as her 'case' against the gods. Finally choosing to put her case in writing, she describes each instance where she has been wronged. It is only after Orual has finished writing that she soberly recognizes her great mistake. To have heard herself making the complaint was to be answered, for she now sees the importance of uttering the speech at the centre of one's soul. She profoundly observes that the gods used her own pen to probe the wounds. With sharpened insight Orual explains. *"Til the words can be dug out of us, why should [the gods] hear the babble that we think we mean? How can they meet us face to face 'til we have faces?"*[42]

Endnotes

1   Jeremiah 29:13, The Holy Bible (NIV). (Nashville, Tennessee: Cornerstone Bible Publishers, 1999).

2   G. K. Chesterton, Ch. 6, "The Paradoxes of Christianity" in *Orthodoxy* (New York: Doubleday, Random House, 2001).

3   A. Lindsley, *True Truth: Defending Absolute Truth in a Relativistic World* (Downers Grove, Illinois: IVP, 2004), 174

4   Brad. J. Kallenberg, *Live to Tell: Evangelism for the Postmodern Age* (Grand Rapids, Michigan: Brazos Press, 2002), 36.

5   Ibid., p.40

6   Chesterton, *Orthodoxy*. 167–168.

7   Ibid., xiii.

8   Corbin Scott Carnell, *Bright Shadow of Reality* (Grand Rapids, Michigan: Erdman's Publishing, 1974), 130–140.

9   Kallenberg, *Live To Tell*, 36.

10   The Book of Mormon, 3 Nephi 27:21 (a distortion of NIV John 13:15: "I have set you an example that you should do as I have done for you").

11   The Holy Bible, Heb 1:1,3.

12   Groat, Joel, Finessing the—God Was Once a Man Like Us. Doctrine http://www.irr.org/mit/finessing-the-god-was-once-a-man.html)

13   Evans, Arza, "Families Held Hostage" in *The Keystone of Mormonism.*, arza@charter.net

14   Ibid.

15   Lavery, Denis., *In the Shadow of the Temple* Anson, Fred. W., https://www.amazon.com/Shadow-Temple-Dennis-Lavery/product-reviews/B002VC7CMO

16   Bruce R. McConkie, *Mormon Doctrine,* third edition (Salt Lake, Utah: Deseret Books, 1978).

17   Chesterton, *Orthodoxy*, 102

18   S.W. Kimball, *The Miracle of Forgiveness* (Salt Lake City, Utah: Bookcraft Inc, 1969), 164–165.

19   Kallenberg, *Live to Tell*, 40.

20 2 Cor 5:21, The Holy Bible, NIV.

21 A. Lindsley, *True Truth: Defending Absolute Truth in a Relativistic World* (Downers Grove, Illinois: IVP, 2004), p174.

22 http://mormonconspiracy.com/mormon-church-lds-conspiracy/2009/01/mormon-church-conspiracy-to-rule-world_13.html

23 Karen E. Rodman (editor), *Asperger's Syndrome and Adults… Is Anyone Listening? Essays and Poems by Partners, Parents and Family Members of Adults with Asperger's Syndrome.* Tony Attwood, Introduction, 42.
     (Jessica Kingsley Pub, 2003).

24 Rodman, *Asperger's Syndrome and Adults,* Tony Attwood, Introduction, 43.

25 Neurotypical, or NT, an abbreviation of *neurologically typical*, is a neologism originating in the autistic community as a label for people who are not on the autism spectrum. Sinclair, Jim (1998). "A note about language and abbreviations." http://web.archive.org/web/20080606024118/http://web.syr.edu/~jisincla/language.htm
     http://jisincla.mysite.syr.edu/

26 Rodman, *Asperger's Syndrome and Adults,* Tony Attwood, Introduction, 42.

27 Ibid., 43.

28 http://www.galaxy.com/rvw23049-586453/FAAAS-Inc-Families-of-Adults-Afflicted-with-Asperger-s-Syndrome-Home-Page.htm

29 Harbinson, *Savage Shepherds.*

30 Ibid., 27.

31 Eliza Doolittle is a fictional character who appears in the play *Pygmalion* (George Bernard Shaw, 1912) and the musical version of that play, *My Fair Lady.*

32 In the play *Pygmalion* (George Bernard Shaw, 1912) and the musical version of that play *My Fair Lady,* Eliza is a Cockney flower girl who comes to Professor Henry Higgins asking for elocution lessons, after a chance encounter at Covent Garden. Higgins goes along with it for the purposes of a wager: that he can turn her into the toast of elite London society.

33 Avoidant: a·void·ant (ə-voidənt)
     adj.—Tending to avoid or shun something, especially as a means of coping with anxiety or stress: risk-avoidant behavior; therapies aimed at socially avoidant children. American Heritage Dictionary of the English Language, Fifth Edition: Houghton Mifflin Harcourt Publishing Company.
     avoidant (əvɔdənt) adj—1. (of behaviour) demonstrating a tendency to avoid intimacy or interaction with others. Collins English Dictionary, Complete and Unabridged. HarperCollins Publishers, 2003. http://www.thefreedictionary.com/avoidant

34 Harbinson, *Savage Shepherds,* 100.

35 Fruzzetti, A.E. & Iversion, 2006. https://thrivingisthegoal.com/tag/aspergating-the-self/ (paraphrased)

36 https://www.theguardian.com/commentisfree/2017/ jan/02/japanese-husband-speak-wife-abuse-coercive-control

37 https://thrivingisthegoal.com/tag/aspergating-the-self/

38 https://www.theguardian.com/science/2017/mar/16/gaslighting-manipulation-reality-coping-mechanisms-trump

39 Juanita. P Lovett, *Solutions for Adults with Asperger Syndrome (Gloucester, MA: Fair Winds Press, 2005), 124–125.*

40 Rodman, *Asperger's Syndrome and Adults*, Tony Attwood, Introduction, 43.

41 Jill Carattini, *A Slice of Infinity*, RZIM, first published *July 12, 2006; re-*published, amended, 15 June 2016. Digging Out the Words.

42 C.S. Lewis, *Til We Have Faces*, quoted by Carattini, Jill, *A Slice of Infinity.*

Printed in the United States
By Bookmasters